From Barriers
to Bridges

May you know the
Grace, Joy +
Infinite Possibilities
of Bridging—It ~

Maria

From Barriers to Bridges

A Treatise

Maria A Rodriguez

BMcTALKS Press
4980 South Alma School Road
Suite 2-493
Chandler, Arizona 85248

Volume pricing is available to bulk orders placed by corporations, associations, and others. For details, please contact BMcTALKS Press at info@bmtpress.com

FIRST EDITION

Paperback (English): 978-1-953315-08-3
eBook (English): 978-1-953315-09-0
Paperback (Spanish): 978-1-953315-12-0
eBook (Spanish): 978-1-953315-13-7

Cover and interior design by Medlar Publishing Solutions Pvt Ltd., India.

Printed in the United States of America.

*Dedicated to
those who are opening to
the purple waves of truth and
love, and of hope and possibility.*

From Barriers to Bridges

A Treatise

Contents

Preface

This sacred text has a will of its own. I have been appointed as Vessel and Guardian. As such, you will find a notable use of capitalization throughout your reading of this text. This format was kept intact in order to honor how this wisdom was originally received. Each capitalized word is meant to emit the transformative power of that quality as you read it. Think of the capitalized elements as active ingredients in a multi-vitamin for your whole being—body, mind, heart, and spirit.

You will also find a tempo and cadence that at times supersedes normally recommended rules of grammar. This was chosen in reverence of what is meant to be transmitted through this text. Reading it aloud can further activate the multi-dimensional nature of the wisdom contained herein.

May this preface serve as encouragement for you too to stay true to the pure nature and creative genius of your own intuitive knowing.

María A Rodríguez

From Barriers to Bridges

From Impasses to Inroads

Whether it's our relationships, our habits, our businesses, or our government- Barriers are dissolving, making way for bridges to be built where barriers once stood. Bridges appearing in the most surprising places.

Bridges between two parts within us that have pulled us in opposite directions for decades, succeeding in keeping us stuck in place:

> *I want freedom and I want security. I love you and I hate you.*
> *I'm good and I'm bad. The World Sucks, The World Wipes.*
> *I'm Hot!, I'm Not!*

Bridges between two souls that have lived the great divide, between two peoples that have hated and have killed.

Bridges between money and soul, between the ME and the WE. Bridges between Truth and Love.

Bridges of Compassion and Creativity.

The two most needed elements on the planet
    The ones that we,
        that you and I and they,
all need.

Compassion and Creativity ~ the most Potent Portents of our Times

Compassion and Creativity ~

the two most needed elements on the planet

We must begin with Compassion. Hold on, hold on, it's not what you think and … it is what you think.

First, let me explain.

We cannot even bring compassion to that which we cannot feel and do not understand. And we cannot feel and understand that which we cannot see or hear.

So we must first

Look Very Closely and Listen Really Well

And yet, this we cannot do within our old Agree/Disagree Paradigm. A paradigm that by its very nature, misses the other hand. Misses an entire half. Misses a whole 50% of the picture, of the story, of what matters, of ourselves. A paradigm that always asks which side are you on: the side of the right or the left, of the administration or the employees, of the husband or the wife, of the us or the them, of the good guys or the bad guys.

Consider This

A friend and I were on a quick phone chat, catching up. He was sharing about moving to a new office space because the university where he worked wasn't doing well. He suddenly became incensed as he declared, "The President is not good for higher education." He went on to explain how the many cuts in financial aid were decreasing attendance. I was immediately struck by something; I wasn't quite sure what. Then I realized that it wasn't what was being said, it was the part that was missing-the pressure and criticism that the President was at that same exact time receiving for the very opposite, not reducing government spending enough.

Look Very Closely
and
Listen Really Well

We can only Look Very Closely and Listen Really Well,
by stepping into the world of 360 degrees–

Into the 360 Degree Paradigm.

Into the world of the Whole Picture,
Into the world of the Full Story,
Into the world of the 100%

Into the space of the In-Between

Consider This

*Soon after the presidential election, after listening to some folks
who voted the same as my husband did voice their reactions, he says
to me, "Funny, you and I (who actually vote for opposing teams)
are far closer than I am to many of those in my own party."*

Then and only then, because of moving into
alignment with Truth, with the Clarity that
comes from the 360° Truth within this paradigm,
we now move out of our many misalignments;
misalignments in attitudes, jobs, perceptions,
relationships, systems, and on and on it goes.

Then and only then can we move into states of being,
into qualities of being, that draw us personally and
collectively onto higher ground. Which truly bless
all that is.

I Choose the 360° Way!

Consider This

360 DEGREE PERSPECTIVE	AGREE/DISAGREE PERSPECTIVE
expands	narrows
firm and flexible	rigid or collapsed
opens us up	closes us off
facing in and out facing up and down	facing on or off
unites (us and them, me and you)	divides (us vs. them, me vs. you)
differentiated	symbiotic
Harmonious, with dialogue and synergistic flow leading to the sacred quandary	Oppositional, with power struggle and debate leading to conflict and impasses
ponders and considers spells it out and checks it out co-discerns and co-creates	avoids and ignores assumes and concludes accepts or rejects
black and white and all shades of gray and colors in between	black or white
both/and	either/or
enhances the center of the circle (or group)- the space "between us"	collapses the center of the circle- the space "between us"
progresses us: we emerge in a new place	stagnates us: we remain in the same place

Check It Out
and
Spell It Out

multi-dimensional: *sees also the level of* *mirror, microcosm, and* *metaphor*	*one-dimensional:* *sees only the level of a single* *fact, suspicion, interpretation,* *and projection*
centered, clear, confident, *curious, and compassionate*	*judgmental, defensive,* *manipulative, or resigned*
undisguised and undefended	*disguised and defended*
humble and assertive *respectful and regardful* *willing and present*	*arrogant and aggressive* *passive and submissive* *resistant and avoidant*
seeks the big "T" Truth, *knowing there is more to* *discover/open to all small "t"* *truths within*	*sees only a few small "t"* *truths, believing they are the* *big "T" Truth/closed off to the* *rest of the Truth*

We often mistake Compassion with an unwillingness to see the truth, with accepting and tolerating that which is unacceptable and intolerable. We mistake Compassion with enabling and prolonging that which is harmful or misaligned.

When in reality, it is the Clarity that only comes from Compassionate eyes (bringing regard and value to all that is, the good the bad the ugly, and everything in between) that leads us to the whole picture and through that, into divine alignment.

When in reality, Compassion is what avoids, ignores, minimizes, maximizes, and distorts *nothing*. When in reality, Compassion is what misses *nothing*.

And for you accountability nuts (how smart you are), compassion holds everyone and everything accountable. Yes… accountable.

Multi-Dimensional~ That's Me!

the Eyes of the Heart see everything

Consider This

Remember a time when you heard someone express what they thought was compassion for another, and yet it was clear that they were actually in denial about that other person-that they were not seeing the whole truth about the other person. Remember the feeling in your body? It was probably tense and uneasy, right?

Now imagine that same scene
but this time they are seeing the gist of everything,
denying and excusing nothing, doing whatever it is that needs to be done,
and yet, at the same time,
blessing the other person with Light, Love and Goodwill.

They are now seeing way beyond the eyes of sympathy or judgment.
They are now standing within boundaries, setting and enforcing them,
boundaries that are the perfect match for all that is,
and yet, at the same time,
blessing the other person with Light, Love and Goodwill.

Now, what is the feeling in your body?
Can you feel it?
The sense of peace
The sense of rightness and goodness for all
The sense of safety and protection
The sense of being beautifully grounded and centered
The sense of being at ease

This is the state of Compassion.
This is the light of Clarity that exists
within Compassion.

the Eyes of the Heart see everything

The Truth is not a matter of opinion

The Truth is not a matter of opinion

The Truth is not a matter of opinion

It is what Is

It   holds   everything   and   everyone   at   once

It cannot be moved
It can only be discovered

It can only be discovered by those who now hear the Call and who now have the Courage to do so.

For when the Truth is what we are tapping into, we all tap into the same thing.

The Same Thing

can you even believe it?

can you dare to believe it?

One by one and two by two, a hundred by a hundred,
we are hearing that *call* and stepping into that *courage*.

It may already be you. It may be about to be you.

the Truth cannot
be moved,

it can only
be Discovered

There are many bridges that can help us cross over into this much needed paradigm. The bridges that have been around forever and the newer ones, springing up all over the place.

For some, it's the bridge of meditation, of prayer, of healing, of therapy, of retreats.

For others, it being out on the golf course on a day when it's okay no matter how we golf.

Children and animals and nature have a way of bringing us here too, along with…

The stories and the storytellers
The artists, the musicians, the writers
The world of science in its infinite nature.

Consider This

"Simply Pause, Pause, Pause
for that Pause alone is Golden"

Simply Pause
whenever you're off and running
about anything or anyone
including yourself
maybe especially yourself
and ask:

WHERE IS THE OTHER HAND?

where oh where is the other hand???

Where oh where is the other hand?

For even if you cannot yet see what's in your blind spot, what is beyond your experience, this other hand
For even if you cannot yet feel it or hear it or touch it or know it,
Just-moving on over... to this new center, as you make room for this missing half, this missing hand
Just-moving on over... into the space that lives in-between the two hands,
Brings you into the perfect spot, the sweet spot, the one that we're all desperate for.

For we no longer need to see and hear and understand and feel and know. Thank you, God.
This bridge of "pausing and asking" brings us right to that sweet spot with the question alone! "Where is the other hand?"
No need for the answer. For we have already been *shifted and transported, shifted and transported,* and then...

And then, we can step right into the world of Creativity.

Yes, Creativity. You've heard of Creative Problem-Solving...
of the real kind.

The *kind* that is not distracted, detoured, or delayed by anything.

The *kind* that doesn't go around and around in circles.

The *kind* that is not closed off to anything.

The *kind* that flows around everywhere,
around the 360 degrees,
not straying too far or too long from the center of it all,
where Balance lives.

For that is where the source of Infinite Creativity lives too.

I am being Shifted and Transported

For that is where the source of Infinite Creativity lives too:

Where the seemingly unsolvable is resolved, dissolved.

Where amazing, miraculous ideas are birthed and brought to fruition.

Where we draw, erase and contemplate... then repeat.

Where we collaborate and cooperate.

Where we face the truths...

the easier ones and the harder ones,
the clearer ones and the confusing ones,
the harmonious ones and the conflicting ones,
the uplifting ones and the heartbreaking ones.

All together in one place.

No one is unwelcomed here,

For here is all that is.

Consider This

A client comes to see me after years of traditional therapy. She has been torn between two men, going around and around and around, yet getting nowhere. I gently tell her that if the answer lay there, she would have found it long ago. As we shifted into this 360-degree paradigm and into the living waters that reside therein, we were led to places in her life story, into the underground world of her

I want to live
where the source of
Infinite Creativity
lives too

psyche, even into the spaces beyond this lifetime, adding many new ingredients to what she already knew was there. She found herself creating a brand-new recipe from what was truly there, blending it together, becoming centered within it, creating a fuller and truer picture that for the very first time allows her, frees her, guides her... right into alignment. And when we are aligned, we bring that energy of alignment to all we touch.

It truly is the Midas Touch.

Alleluia!

This client at various times said to me things like "You are a genius;" "You are a miracle worker." Each time I smiled. Each time I gave a silent bow of gratitude for all of what and all of whom have led me, before I came to lead her and others, to the center of this (w)holy paradigm. Where the genius of Truth lies, and where miracles do occur.

Maybe she too will become an ambassador, a humble advocate, of All Of This.

With Compassion and through Creativity we are brought to the very edge of Alignment. Let us end this Treatise with this:

ALIGN
ALIGN
ALIGN

*for even the smallest
of misalignments has
the greatest of effects*

Consider This

---

*I am meeting with a client when the next thing I know, I am standing
up, relaying a message in a booming voice, coming from God only
knows where:*

"ALIGN

ALIGN

ALIGN

for even the smallest of misalignments,
has the greatest of effects."

*I sit back down, both of us stunned at the power of these words,
at the might of this message... becoming even more blessed,
as it fully sinks in.*

Alignment, Full-Being Alignment, Full-World Alignment.
One of the many golden treasures we find,
one of many things that become possible as we shift into
Compassion and Creativity.
For that is what the Bridges are made of.
And yet, we are only brought to the edge of Alignment
through Compassion and Creativity. We must choose to Align, and
then Align, and then Align some more.

With every step, with every new alignment,
the Bridges become longer and stronger, stronger and longer.

Full-Being Alignment

Full-World Alignment

From Barriers to Bridges

From Impasses to Inroads

From MisAlignment to Alignment:

A Treatise

by Maria A Rodriguez

From Barriers to Bridges

A Treatise in the Making

After a long morning of capturing yet another mystical, magical story which had occurred weeks earlier, a story about a lost and then found money clip, both lost and found in quite dramatic ways, I was all written out... or so I thought. It was as if from pushing out that entire story, a void had been created within me, and this just couldn't wait to pour in. And pour in it did.

I leave my office, get in the car, worrying about the time, thinking of the many errands I still needed to run, and deciding "first stop Ulta" since I was out of one of my hair products and didn't want to forget. As I pull out of my parking space, my mind continues along this vein: what should I cook for dinner?, Oh, I need to make that return at Target....

I don't even make it out of the parking lot when from somewhere outside of my chattering mind, I hear, "*Compassion and Creativity–the two most needed elements on the planet.*" What?!! And it continued, "*We cannot bring compassion to that which we cannot feel and do not understand; we cannot feel and understand that which we cannot see or hear.*" On and on it went.

I truly don't know how I made it to Ulta. I park abruptly, desperate to get to my iPhone, and begin typing typing typing. I couldn't type quite fast enough to keep up with the voice. When it was over, stunned, my thumbs sore, I look up, not sure where I was or what I was doing there. First thing I see is Ulta. And then it all came back to me. What the heck was that?!, I think to myself. "*A Treatise,*" I hear. Yep, that's right. I got an actual answer!

Well, what the heck is a treatise? My only sense of it was as vague as it was in the distant past.... from maybe a Poli Sci class. Oh wait, it didn't say Treaty; it said Treatise. And to think how bizarre I had found the money clip story from that morning. Now a treatise of all things!

And so, of course, I had to look up Treatise, pretty easy since I'm a teeny bit addicted to my Merriam Webster Dictionary app. It says, *"A Treatise is a systematic exposition or argument in writing including a methodical discussion of the facts and principles involved and conclusions reached."* Huh? Well, it certainly had an air about it that was a different style of writing for me. And there were facts and principles and conclusions. But "systematic and methodical" and a strange voice, mad drive, Ulta parking lot, iPhone writing sprint don't seem to have much in common. Oh well, a treatise they said it was so a Treatise it is.

I had assumed that the title was "Compassion and Creativity: A Treatise" since that's how it had begun. But then, my monthly training group (hmmm, how to describe it... something like "Archetypes R Us") was having its final gathering and holiday party. At one point, one of the gals and I were sitting together on the couch, marveling at some healing that was occurring where there had been tension in the group. At the very same moment she was saying, "Barriers are dissolving," I was saying, "Bridges are being built." We froze, staring at each other, overcome by the sacred power suddenly surrounding us. Then I say, "Barriers and Bridges, Bridges and Barriers...From Barriers to Bridges." She didn't even bother to ask what I was talking about since it was already, just too much.

Later as I get in my car to head home (I know, me behind the wheel is getting a bit scary now, right), I hear, *"From Barriers to Bridges: A Treatise."* What?! Oh, that's right, that strange thing I had written in the Ulta parking lot. I guess I'm being shown I had gotten the title wrong! Wow. Okay. I then feel more coming through. And then, you guessed it, driving home, I hear, *"From Barriers to Bridges, from Impasses to Inroads..."* and at a short jog thankfully rather than that earlier marathon sprint, I hear the rest of the true opening passage of this Treatise.

I pull in my driveway, get my handy dandy iPhone out, and jot it all down. I don't know what it was...something about this new opening. I was beginning to get it, to get it in a sobering reality kind of way. In a take-my-breath-away kind of way. In a "This Is Big" kind of way. This is really, really Big. And it must be done. I must find a way to get this out. I must find a way.

So here we are. Me introducing this Treatise. And You helping me get it out. Many, many thanks. Really. Really.

Maria

About Maria

Maria A Rodriguez is a clinical social worker turned evolutionary revolutionary. She began her career as a police social worker and community leader, serving the many impacted by domestic violence, family turmoil, mental illness, and traumatic death. While in the midst of her own transformational healing in an intensive couple's therapy training program, spiritual forces blew into her life, changing the course of her life forever. She underwent a major relationship change, an unexpected turn in her career, and a profound spiritual awakening.

These mystical happenings continued when Maria was jolted awake to the words "Sacred Spaces — within us, between us, around us," a new name and unique direction for her private practice. Her sense of wholeness and aliveness grew as she became further aligned with her path, passion, and purpose. During a challenging client session, she began receiving a profoundly liberating body of wisdom, guiding us in "Breaking our Toxic Shame Cycles." A model for "Leading a Spirit-Driven Life" also emerged, helping us to access and live in alignment with our soul's guidance.

Over time, this evolved into "Seven Bridges to Higher Consciousness" with additional fundamental shifts to our way of thinking, being, living and relating. She developed Cour de Grace, LLC as an online forum to further her dream of an evolution revolution, based on these enlightened and empowering paradigms for living. She envisions a wisdom school and social movement, leading to a world where these become our mainstream mindsets and skill sets. Maria is devoted to healing ourselves, our relationships, our systems, and our communities, thus, unleashing the power of grace in the world.